BOSTON
RED SOX

by Lew Freedman

Published by ABDO Publishing Company, 8000 West 78th Street, Edina, Minnesota 55439. Copyright © 2011 by Abdo Consulting Group, Inc. International copyrights reserved in all countries. No part of this book may be reproduced in any form without written permission from the publisher. SportsZone™ is a trademark and logo of ABDO Publishing Company.

Printed in the United States of America,
North Mankato, Minnesota
112010
012011

Editor: Chrös McDougall
Copy Editor: Nicholas Cafarelli
Interior Design and Production: Carol Castro
Cover Design: Kazuko Collins

Photo Credits: Mary Schwalm/AP Images, cover; Paul Benoit/AP Images, 1; Julie Jacobson/AP Images, 4, Elise Amendola/AP Images, 7; Mark Humphrey/ AP Images, 9, 43 (middle); George Grantham Bain/Library of Congress, 10, 42 (top); Harris & Ewing/Library of Congress, 12; AP Images, 14, 17, 42 (middle), 18, 21, 29, 31, 37; Green/AP Images, 22; AP Images, 24, 42 (bottom); Frank C. Curtin/AP Images, 26; Harry Cabluck/AP Images, 32, 43 (top); Peter Southwick/ AP Images, 34; Charles Krupa/AP Images, 38; Darren Calabrese/The Canadian Press/AP Images, 41, 43 (bottom); Ted Mathias/AP Images, 44; Robert Cohen/ St. Louis Post-Dispatch/AP Images, 47

Library of Congress Cataloging-in-Publication Data
Freedman, Lew.
  Boston Red Sox / by Lew Freedman.
    p. cm. — (Inside MLB)
  Includes index.
  ISBN 978-1-61714-037-2
  1. Boston Red Sox (Baseball team)—History—Juvenile literature. I. Title.
  GV875.B62F725 2011
  796.357'640974461—dc22
                                    2010036554

TABLE OF CONTENTS

CHAPTER 1

CHAMPS AT LAST

It was never going to happen. Most Boston Red Sox fans had accepted it by 2004. The Red Sox had won five World Series titles between 1903 and 1918. Then they sold slugger Babe "The Bambino" Ruth to the rival New York Yankees in 1920. They had not won a World Series since. As for the hated Yankees: They won 26 titles from 1920 through 2004. It was called the Curse of the Bambino.

The "curse" was in full effect for the 2003 American League (AL) playoffs. After each won in the AL Division Series (ALDS), the Red Sox and the Yankees met in the AL Championship Series (ALCS) to determine who went to the World Series.

It was a back-and-forth series. Every game except one was decided by three runs or less. After six games, the Red Sox and Yankees had each won three. It would all come down to the decisive seventh game at Yankee Stadium in New York.

Manny Ramirez, *left*, and David Ortiz celebrate after Ortiz hit a two-run homer against the New York Yankees in the 2004 ALCS.

The Red Sox took a 5–2 lead in the top of the eighth inning and appeared to be on their way to the World Series. Then the curse struck. Boston's ace pitcher, Pedro Martinez, gave up three runs in the bottom of the eighth. The game was still tied going into the bottom of the 11th inning. Then Yankees third baseman Aaron Boone hit a solo home run to left field. The Yankees had done it again.

The "Idiots"

The Red Sox and the Yankees were rivals on the field. They also had very different personas off it. The Yankees were known for their corporate image. All the players were neat and clean shaven. The Red Sox were the opposite. Outfielder Johnny Damon was the most obvious example. His long brown hair and scruffy beard in 2004 made him look like a caveman. Damon referred to the 2004 Red Sox as "the idiots" to show that they were just regular, fun-loving guys who loved to play baseball.

The Red Sox were back in 2004. They finished the regular season with a 98–64 record and qualified for the playoffs as the wild card. Behind pitchers Curt Schilling, Martinez, Bronson Arroyo, and Derek Lowe, the Red Sox then blew through the Anaheim Angels in the ALDS. Next up was a rematch with the Yankees.

Any optimism in Boston faded quickly when the ALCS started. The Yankees jumped to a three-games-to-none lead in the series. The third was a crushing 19–8 win at Boston's Fenway Park. In more than 100 years of Major League Baseball history, no team had ever won a seven-game series after losing the first three games. When the Yankees took a 4–3 lead into the bottom of the ninth inning of Game 4, the Curse of the Bambino appeared to have struck again.

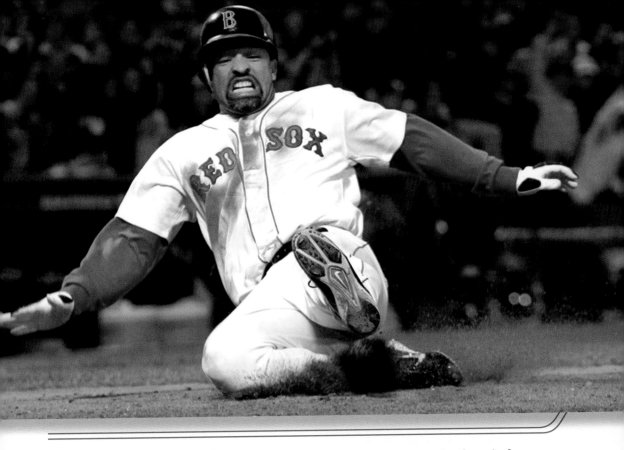

Dave Roberts slides into home plate to score the tying run in the ninth inning of Game 4 in the 2004 ALCS.

Then something amazing happened. Yankees ace closer Mariano Rivera walked Red Sox first baseman Kevin Millar. Moments later, pinch runner Dave Roberts stole second base. When third baseman Bill Mueller singled to center, Roberts touched home for the tying run. The Red Sox were back in it.

The game went into extra innings. Finally, in the bottom of the 12th, Boston's powerful designated hitter David Ortiz blasted a two-run home run to give the Red Sox the win. They would live another day.

The Red Sox then edged the Yankees 5–4 after 14 innings in Game 5. The series returned to

THE BLOODY SOCK

Red Sox pitcher Curt Schilling was on the mound during Game 6 of the 2004 ALCS when a red splotch appeared on his right sock. It was blood. An ankle injury had hurt him in Game 1, when he gave up six earned runs in three innings. But doctors temporarily stitched it up and he was back on the mound for Game 6. In a legendary performance, Schilling gave up one run in seven innings while blood seeped out of his ankle. The win helped force the seventh game. Schilling overcame a bloody sock again in Game 2 of the World Series. He pitched six innings while giving up no earned runs in the win.

Schilling's bloody socks became a symbol of the 2004 Red Sox's grit and determination as they won their first World Series title in 86 years. Schilling donated the second bloody sock to the Baseball Hall of Fame in 2005.

Yankee Stadium for Game 6. But the result was the same: Boston won 4–2. It would all come down to Game 7 in New York. The Red Sox took any drama out of this one, though. They crushed the Yankees 10–3.

Finally, after so many heartbreaking losses to the Yankees, the Red Sox had won in the biggest way. But Red Sox fans were not ready to celebrate just yet. The National League (NL) champion St. Louis Cardinals awaited in the World Series.

After the Red Sox's dramatic comeback in the ALCS, they were not going to be stopped in the World Series. Outfielder Manny Ramirez batted .412 and had four runs batted in (RBIs). Pitchers Schilling, Martinez, and Lowe completely silenced the Cardinals batters. The three

Pokey Reese jumps on top of his teammates as the Red Sox celebrate their 2004 World Series title. It was Boston's first title since 1918.

starters gave up a combined zero earned runs in 20 innings. The Red Sox swept the Cardinals in four games. After 86 years, the curse had finally been reversed.

"When somebody tells you that you can't do something that you think you can, given an opportunity, you want to go out there and prove to yourself that you can do it," Lowe said.

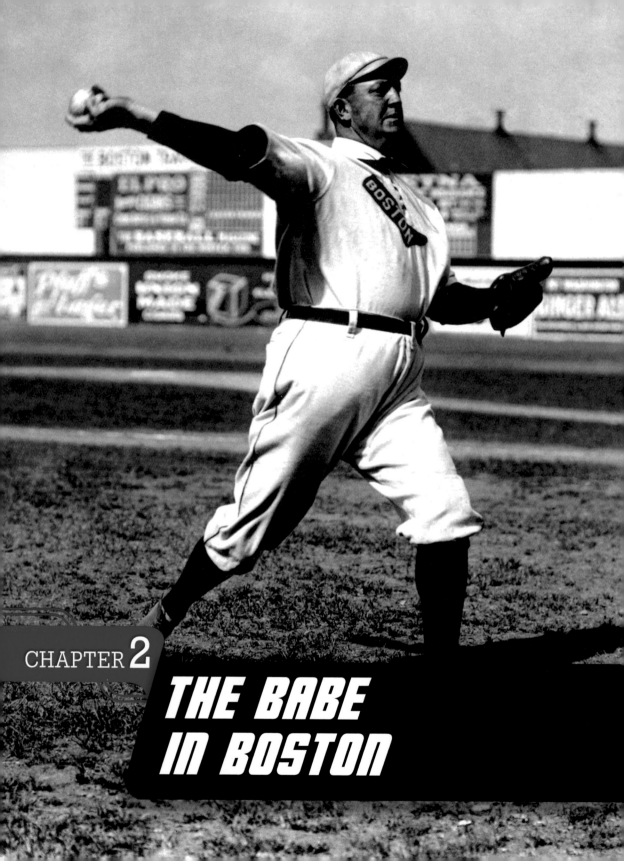

CHAPTER 2

THE BABE IN BOSTON

Boston's professional baseball team began as an original member of the AL when the league formed in 1901. At the time, the team was known as the Boston Americans. It was not until 1908 that the team became officially known as the Red Sox.

The Americans' first game was a loss to the Orioles in Baltimore on April 26, 1901. However, they finished the season second in the AL with a 79–57 record. One of those wins was against the Orioles on July 3. Americans pitcher Cy Young recorded his 300th career win that day. That number is now a benchmark for determining great pitchers.

Young was the Americans' first ace. He won an average of 24 games with a 2.00 earned-run average (ERA) during his eight seasons in Boston. In 1903, he also helped the Americans win

Cy Young, shown pitching for the Red Sox in 1908, helped the Boston Americans win their first World Series title in 1903.

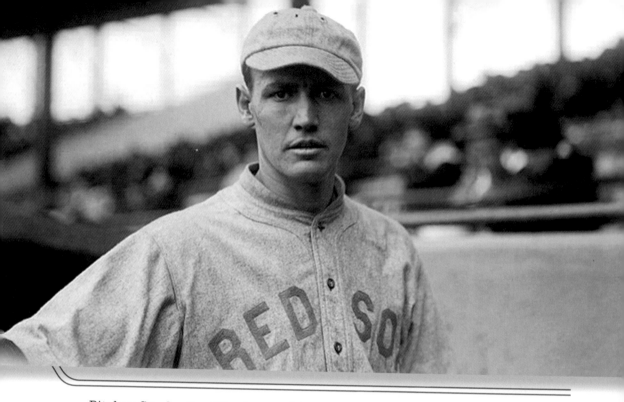

Pitcher Smoky Joe Wood went 34–5 with a 1.91 ERA in 1912 for the Red Sox.

Cy Young

Denton True Young got the nick-name Cy after he threw a baseball into a fence so hard that it looked like damage from a cyclone. By the end of his 22-year career, Cy Young was a name synonymous with great pitching. The farm boy from Ohio won 511 games during his career—the next best is Walter Johnson, who won 417. Today, the Cy Young Award is given to the best pitcher in each league after the season.

their first World Series. Young gave up only seven earned runs in 34 innings as Boston defeated the Pittsburgh Pirates five games to three.

Young left Boston after the 1908 season. But the Red Sox remained a top team thanks to the addition of some talented players. Outfielder Tris Speaker came aboard in 1907. Ace pitcher Smoky Joe Wood joined the team in 1908. The Red Sox then added star outfielders Harry Hooper in 1909 and Duffy Lewis in 1910.

Those players led the Red Sox to another memorable season in 1912. The team moved into Fenway Park that year. It is still the Red Sox's home stadium today. They had previously played home games in a wooden ballpark called the Huntington Avenue Grounds.

Wood was dominant during the 1912 regular season. He finished 34–5 with a 1.91 ERA. It was one of the best single-season pitching performances ever. The Red Sox capped the season off with a 4–3–1 World Series win over the New York Giants. One of the games was a tie, so the teams had to play a deciding eighth game.

All four players were back in 1915 and helped the Red Sox defeat the Philadelphia Phillies 4–1 in the World Series. By then, the Red Sox were also seeing the emergence of another future star player.

Babe Ruth made his major league debut with the Red Sox in 1914. Although he was later known for his powerful batting, Ruth began as a top left-handed pitcher. He won 18 games with a 2.44 ERA in 1915. However, he did not pitch in that year's World Series.

The Royal Rooters

The Red Sox were one of the first teams with an organized fan club. A group called the Royal Rooters sat together at the Huntington Avenue Grounds. They made their first road trip in 1903 when they traveled to Pittsburgh for the World Series.

The Royal Rooters were also famous for their singing of the song "Tessie." They soon turned the Broadway musical song into the Red Sox's theme song. In 2004, local rock band The Dropkick Murphys remade "Tessie" and it again became a hit among Red Sox fans.

Outfielders, *from left*, Duffy Lewis, Tris Speaker, and Harry Hooper, guided the Red Sox to two World Series titles from 1910 to 1915.

Speaker and Wood left after the 1915 season, but Boston kept winning. Ruth won 23 games as a pitcher in 1916. He then pitched a 14-inning complete game in the World Series. Ruth only gave up one run in the 2–1 win over the Brooklyn Robins. The Red Sox went on to beat the Robins in five games.

Lewis left the Red Sox after the 1917 season. But by 1918, Ruth was emerging as a top batter as well as a top pitcher. He drove in a team-high 66 runs despite only batting part-time. He cut back his pitching too, but still won 13 games while keeping a 2.22 ERA. The Red Sox went to their fifth World

Series after that season. Once again, Ruth was great.

The 23-year-old Ruth had only one hit in five at-bats against the Chicago Cubs in the World Series. But that hit was a triple that drove in two runs. And he was dominant on the mound. Ruth won both of his starts and finished with a 1.06 ERA. He also extended his World Series scoreless streak to 29 2/3 innings. That record stood until 1961. The Red Sox defeated the Cubs four games to two.

Life was good in Boston. The Red Sox had won five World Series titles in only 16 years. They also had one of the best young players in baseball in Ruth. But soon things began to change.

Ruth had shown a lot of ability as a batter. In 1919, he continued his transition from starting pitcher to outfielder.

Ruth batted .322 with 114 RBIs—by far the most on the team. Although he only pitched in 17 games, Ruth still won nine of them. But the Red Sox did not play well as a team. They went 66–71 and dropped to sixth in the AL.

By 1920, Ruth had established himself as one of the best players in the game. As such, he wanted to be paid more. But

Million-Dollar Outfield

The "Million-Dollar Outfield" consisted of Tris Speaker, Harry Hooper, and Duffy Lewis. Speaker is considered one of the greatest fielding center fielders of all time. He also had a .345 lifetime batting average. Hooper was a noted leadoff man who still owns Red Sox records for triples and stolen bases. Lewis was also among the league's best hitters at the time. Both Speaker and Hooper were later enshrined in the Hall of Fame. The Million-Dollar Outfield was together from 1910 to 1915 and helped the Red Sox win two World Series titles.

A STRANGE YEAR

The Red Sox won their fifth World Series title in 1918. The triumph was recorded in an unusual baseball year. The world was embroiled in World War I at the time. In cooperation with the federal government, baseball administrators cut the season short after the United States entered the conflict. The Red Sox played 126 games instead of the full 154 games in 1918.

The Red Sox still had a great season. They had clinched the AL pennant by the end of August and prepared to meet the Chicago Cubs in the World Series. But the war had distracted baseball fans, and attendance had dropped significantly. The team owners lowered ticket prices to attract crowds, but they did so at the expense of the players' World Series bonuses. The angry players demanded more money. There was worry that fans might start a riot. But ultimately the games were played peacefully.

the Red Sox balked at Ruth's salary demands. Instead, they sold him to the New York Yankees for $125,000.

The Yankees had struggled during their first 19 seasons, never reaching the World Series. The Red Sox, on the other hand, had been one of the best teams in baseball. Red Sox owner Harry Frazee figured the Yankees would continue to struggle by having to deal with Ruth's high salary. Meanwhile, his Red Sox could use the money to rebuild and win more World Series titles. Instead, it turned out to be quite the opposite.

Babe Ruth made his major league debut with the Red Sox in 1914 as a top pitcher. He became known as the "Sultan of Swat" when he played outfield for the New York Yankees.

CHAPTER 3

BIG STARS IN LEAN YEARS

As it turned out, Red Sox owner Harry Frazee was more interested in producing Broadway plays than rebuilding his championship baseball club.

After selling Babe Ruth, Frazee continued selling the Red Sox's other top players. The Red Sox quickly became the worst team in the AL. They finished last in the league nine times from 1922 through 1932. The worst was 1932, when they finished a dismal 43–111. Ruth and the Yankees, meanwhile, went to seven World Series and won four of them between 1921 and 1932.

It took until the mid 1930s before the Red Sox showed signs of coming back. That was largely because of new owner Thomas J. Yawkey. Yawkey's uncle had owned the Detroit Tigers. From his uncle, Yawkey inherited $40 million and a love for baseball. Yawkey bought

First baseman Jimmie Foxx, *left*, poses with his new manager and teammate Joe Cronin at spring training in 1936.

To the Hall

The Red Sox added Lefty Grove in 1934, Joe Cronin in 1935, and Jimmie Foxx in 1936. All three were later selected to the Hall of Fame. Grove stayed in Boston until he retired after the 1941 season. He compiled a 105–62 record during that time. Cronin retired as a Red Sox player in 1945. Foxx left Boston during the 1942 season and retired in 1945. After 20 seasons he had 534 home runs. Only Babe Ruth had more at the time. Another future Hall of Fame player, catcher Rick Ferrell, played in Boston from 1933 to 1937.

the Red Sox for $1.2 million in 1933. He owned the team for the next 43 years.

Yawkey soon began investing large sums of money in the team. He renovated and expanded Fenway Park. One of the most noticeable changes was adding the famous left-field wall now known as "the Green Monster." Yawkey also spent money to add more talented players to his team.

The first big addition to the Red Sox was pitcher Lefty Grove. He came to Boston in 1934 after having won a Most Valuable Player (MVP) Award with the Philadelphia Athletics. Shortstop Joe Cronin came to Boston in 1935. He had previously been an All-Star with the Washington Senators. Then, in 1936, the Red Sox bought Athletics first baseman Jimmie Foxx. He was a two-time MVP and known for his massive home runs.

Despite his tendency to yell at teammates, Grove became a 300-game winner. His finest season for Boston was in 1935, when he finished 20–12. But it was not until 1938 that the Red Sox once again rejoined the AL's elite with a second-place finish.

Foxx won his third MVP Award during that 1938 season. That was the same season that

Hall of Famer Lefty Grove was the first big addition to the Boston Red Sox after the Green Monster was built in 1934.

young second baseman Bobby Doerr broke into the lineup full-time, too. He soon became an annual All-Star. His slick fielding combined with Cronin's to make for a great double-play combination.

"I liked to field," Doerr said. "When I was a boy I'd throw a rubber ball against the front step of my porch and react to what the ball did."

The Red Sox finished second again in 1939. Although they missed out on the World Series, the Red Sox had reason to be excited in 1939. A 20-year-old outfielder named Ted Williams broke in with the team in April of that year.

Center fielder Dom DiMaggio missed three seasons while serving in World War II but was a seven-time All-Star during his 11 years in Boston.

Little Brother

Dom was the youngest of three DiMaggio brothers who all reached the major leagues. The most famous was Yankees outfielder Joe DiMaggio. Although overshadowed by Joe, Dom DiMaggio had a good career. He was a seven-time All-Star and had a career .298 batting average. He also once had a 34-game hitting streak. Had he not missed three seasons while serving in World War II, Dom might have had a shot at the Hall of Fame.

Williams was considered a hitting prodigy. The 6-foot-3, 205-pound player had supreme confidence and studied batting scientifically. When he retired after 19 seasons in Boston, many considered him to be the best hitter ever. Some of his teammates disliked Williams. They thought he was arrogant. But despite what they thought of Williams, he backed up his confidence at the plate. "If there was ever a man born to be a hitter, it was me," he said.

Yet, the Red Sox only won one pennant during Williams's time with the team. In 1946, they went 104–50 to run away with the league title. It was their first since 1918. The Red Sox then faced the NL-champion St. Louis Cardinals in the World Series.

Williams came into the World Series with an inflamed elbow. He had earlier been hit by a pitch in an exhibition game. The Cardinals also did their part to slow him down. Williams, a left-handed hitter, was known for hitting the ball to right field. So the Cardinals stacked their defense in what came to be called "The Williams Shift." The Cardinals' outfielders were positioned far more to their left than normal.

The shortstop played on the same side of second base as the second baseman. The result was Williams getting only five hits—all singles—in 25 World Series at-bats.

Still, the Series came down to the seventh game. But the Cardinals ended up winning after Hall of Famer Enos Slaughter ran all the way from first to home on a double by

Hitting .400

Entering the last day of the 1941 season, Ted Williams was batting .3996. That rounded off officially to a .400 average. Red Sox manager Joe Cronin asked Williams if he wanted to sit out the scheduled doubleheader. That would ensure Williams would hit .400. But Williams said he wanted to earn the .400 average the right way. Philadelphia Athletics manager Connie Mack ordered his staff to try its hardest to get Williams out. In a finish that enhanced his reputation, Williams got six hits in eight at-bats that day and raised his average to .406. He had achieved his milestone.

24   BOSTON RED SOX

Harry Walker in the eighth inning. That broke a 3–3 tie.

The Red Sox came close to the World Series again in 1948. They finished the season tied for first place in the AL with the Cleveland Indians. But the Indians won a one-game play-off to break the tie. Had the Red Sox won, they would have faced the NL-champion Boston Braves in an all-Boston World Series.

Another two decades would pass before the Red Sox made it back to the World Series. Williams and all of his 1940s-era teammates would be long retired by then.

Ted Williams finished the 1941 season with a .406 batting average. No player in the major leagues has hit .400 or better since.

TEDDY BALLGAME

Ted Williams grew up in San Diego and signed with the Red Sox in 1936. He debuted with the big-league team in 1939 and played in Boston through the 1960 season. However, he missed three seasons due to military service. Williams, a pilot, flew many dangerous missions during World War II and the Korean War.

Williams was known for meticulously studying the art of hitting. During his Hall of Fame career, the left-handed swinging Williams was a 17-time All-Star, compiled a .344 lifetime batting average, hit 521 home runs, and drove in 1,839 runs. Williams's on-base percentage of .482 is the best in baseball history. In 1941, Williams batted .406. He was the last player to top the .400 mark.

"Baseball is the only field of endeavor where a man can succeed three times out of ten and be considered a good performer," Williams said.

CHAPTER 4

THE IMPOSSIBLE DREAM

The Red Sox continued to add star players after falling short of the 1946 World Series. In 1947, they brought in pitcher Mel Parnell. He won 123 games and is considered one of the best pitchers in team history. But injuries cut his career short. He retired after the 1956 season, having never finished better than second in the AL.

The team signed Harry Agganis in 1952. He had been a multisport star at Boston University. "The Golden Greek" broke in with the Red Sox in 1954. He was beginning to show some promise in 1955 when he caught pneumonia. Agganis briefly rejoined the team, but then had a relapse. He died at age 26 from a pulmonary embolism, shattering the team's morale.

Third baseman Frank Malzone gave the Red Sox some hope in the late 1950s and early 1960s. He was a six-time All-Star and provided some

Third baseman Frank Malzone brought hope to the Red Sox, but he never experienced the postseason despite six All-Star seasons.

TONY C

The Red Sox signed local teenager Tony Conigliaro in 1962. They hoped he would be a star player for many years. It began well for the player nicknamed Tony C. As a 19-year-old rookie he hit .290 and 24 home runs in 1964. One year later he became the youngest player to lead the AL in home runs when he hit 32. But in 1967, California Angels pitcher Jack Hamilton threw a fastball that hit Conigliaro in the cheek and eye.

Conigliaro missed the entire 1968 season, then came back with solid seasons in 1969 and 1970. But the Red Sox traded him to the Angels in 1971, and he struggled. He later went into a career as a TV sports-caster, but suffered a heart attack and later a stroke. He spent his last eight years on life-support systems before dying in 1990 at age 45. His career and life are among the great tragedies in Red Sox history.

much-needed power to the lineup. But he, too, retired in 1966, having never experienced the postseason.

"The whole 11 years I was in the big leagues, I enjoyed every minute of it," Malzone said. "I wish I had got a chance to play in the postseason."

But there was hope. A 21-year-old outfielder named Carl Yastrzemski had debuted for the Red Sox in 1961. He took over left field for Ted Williams, who had retired the previous season. "Yaz" showed improvement throughout his early years. But in 1966, the team was still struggling. The Red Sox finished 72–90 that season, good for ninth place in the 10-team AL. They were 100-to-1 long shots to win the 1967 pennant.

But that is exactly what they did. Yastrzemski led the AL in hits (189), runs (112),

Fans hoped Carl Yastrzemski, *left*, and Tony Conigliaro could bring the Red Sox another World Series title.

home runs (44), RBIs (121), and batting average (.326) in 1967. Leading the league in batting average, RBIs, and home runs at the end of a season is called the Triple Crown. Through the 2010 season, Yastrzemski is the last one to do it. "Yaz" was also named the AL MVP. Meanwhile, pitcher Jim Lonborg won the AL Cy Young Award with a 22–9 record and an AL-best 246 strikeouts.

Yaz

Carl Yastrzemski did his best to replace Ted Williams as the Red Sox's left fielder. Yaz was an 18-time All-Star during his 23 seasons—all with the Red Sox. He had 1,816 runs, 3,419 hits, 1,844 RBIs, and 452 home runs during his Hall of Fame career. But Yaz was at his best during the 1967 Impossible Dream season. He often came up with clutch hits, and he batted .523 over the last two weeks of the season. He was also a very popular player, and many companies hired him to endorse their products.

Behind Yastrzemski and Lonborg, the Red Sox finished 92–70 in 1967. They edged the Minnesota Twins on the final game of the season to win the AL pennant by one game. That season became known as the "Impossible Dream."

But to truly cap off the Impossible Dream, the Red Sox needed to beat the St. Louis Cardinals in the World Series. That was easier said than done, especially against Cardinals ace Bob Gibson. Lonborg was unavailable for Game 1 after pitching the final game of the regular season. The Red Sox fell just short against Gibson, losing 2–1.

Lonborg was back for Game 2, and Boston won 5–0. But St. Louis came back to win the next two. Lonborg was lights-out again as the Red Sox won Game 5. Then Yastrzemski went 3-for-4 with two runs as Boston won Game 6. But it was not to be. Lonborg came back to pitch in Game 7 on only two days of rest. However, Gibson and the Cardinals easily won the clincher 7–2.

The Red Sox were unable to build upon the Impossible Dream season. They moved back to the middle of the pack in the AL for the next seven seasons. Lonborg left after 1971. However, a new star was emerging in catcher Carlton

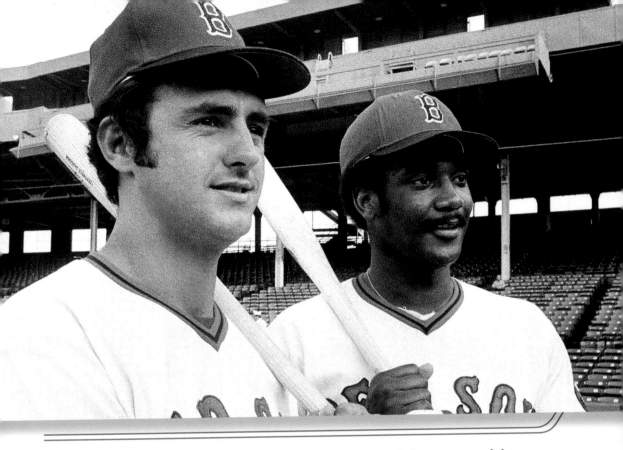

Outfielders Fred Lynn, *left*, and Jim Rice gave the Red Sox a powerful punch in 1975. It was the rookie season for both players.

Fisk. He became a regular in 1972, hitting .293 with 22 home runs and 61 RBIs.

By 1975, the Red Sox were back on top. Outfielder Fred Lynn became the first player to ever win the Rookie of the Year and MVP awards in the same season. Fisk and future Hall of Fame outfielder Jim Rice also had great seasons. With a 95–65 record, the Red Sox won the AL East Division. After sweeping the Oakland Athletics in three games in the ALCS, the Red Sox were headed back to the World Series.

The 1975 Fall Classic turned out to be one for the ages. The Red Sox faced a tough

Carlton Fisk reacts after hitting a 12th-inning home run to lift the Red Sox to a victory in Game 6 of the 1975 World Series.

opponent in the Cincinnati Reds. Both teams were stocked with talented players. And both teams showed up playing their best in the World Series.

It began as a close, back-and-forth Series. The Reds held a 3–2 series lead after five games. Their meeting at Fenway Park for Game 6 became an epic. Because of rain, the sixth game took place five days after the fifth game. That gave the pitchers extra time to recover. Boston sent ace Luis Tiant to the mound to face the Reds' Gary Nolan.

The Red Sox started things off with a three-run first inning. But the Reds came back. They tied it up in the fifth, and then took a 6–3 lead in the top of the eighth. With two men on and two outs in the bottom of the eighth, the Red Sox called on pinch-hitter Bernie Carbo. He had already made himself a folk hero by hitting a pinch-hit home run in Game 3. Then he did it again in Game 6. The Red Sox had tied it up.

The score held until the bottom of the 12th inning. Then Fisk came to the plate. The Red Sox catcher blasted a hit down the left-field line. As the ball hung in the air, Fisk danced on the first-base line, waving his arms to the right as if to keep the ball fair. The ball did stay fair. It bounced off the foul pole for a home run. The Red Sox had survived another day, and it was on to Game 7.

That was the high point of the World Series for the Red Sox. The Big Red Machine, as

Bucky Dent

The Red Sox appeared on their way to another postseason after a 62–28 start in 1978. But a second-half collapse combined with a Yankees' surge left the two rivals tied at 99–63 for first in the AL East. They met at Fenway Park for a one-game playoff. Boston took a 2–0 lead into the seventh inning. Yankees shortstop Bucky Dent averaged five home runs during his 12 major league seasons. But with two men on, he hit one over the Green Monster. Both teams added two more runs, but the Yankees held on to win 5–4.

the Reds were called in those days, came back strong in Game 7. They scored the go-ahead run in the top of the ninth inning to beat the Red Sox 4–3 in Fenway Park. It was not the result that Red Sox fans had hoped for. But they could take solace in knowing their team played hard in one of the most competitive World Series of all time.

CHAPTER 5

BACK AMONG THE BEST

Red Sox fans were used to heartbreak by 1986. After losing in the 1975 World Series, the team had faded back into the middle of the pack. Entering the 1986 season, it had been 68 years since their last World Series title. But behind young fire-throwing pitcher Roger Clemens and sweet-swinging third baseman Wade Boggs, there was hope.

The Red Sox won the AL East. Then they faced the California Angels in the ALCS. The Angels jumped out to a 3–1 series lead. Then, in Game 5, they held a 5–2 lead entering the ninth inning. But the Red Sox were not done.

Sluggers Don Baylor and Dave Henderson each hit home runs to give Boston a 6–5 lead. The Angels then tied it up in the bottom of the inning. But Henderson hit a sacrifice fly to score the winning run in the 11th. The Red Sox then rolled

Hall of Famer Wade Boggs won four consecutive batting titles from 1985 to 1988. He played for the Red Sox from 1982 to 1992.

through Games 6 and 7 to reach their ninth World Series.

The New York Mets had won 108 games that season and were heavily favored in the World Series. But behind strong pitching, Boston won the first two games and held a 3–2 lead after five. Game 6 was dramatic. Boston twice took the lead, only for the Mets to come back and tie it up. Finally, in the top of the 10th, the Red Sox scored two runs to take a 5–3 lead. Their first World Series title in 68 years was only three outs away.

After getting two outs in the bottom of the inning, the Red Sox came within one strike of the World Series title. But then it all fell apart.

First, Mets catcher Gary Carter hit a single. Then pinch-hitter Kevin Mitchell singled, advancing Carter to second. Then, with two strikes, Mets third baseman Ray Knight drove Carter home with a single to center. Mitchell advanced to third on the play. Then he scored the tying run when Red Sox pitcher Bob Stanley threw a wild pitch.

Stanley battled Mets left fielder Mookie Wilson to a full count. Finally, on the 10th pitch, Wilson made contact. It was a routine ground ball to first base. But Red Sox first

Strikeout King

Roger "Rocket" Clemens electrified Red Sox fans as a young player. On April 29, 1986, the fastball specialist struck out 20 Seattle Mariners in one game. That set a major league record. On September 18, 1996, Clemens did it again against the Detroit Tigers.

Clemens debuted as a 21-year-old in 1984. He stayed in Boston through 1996. During that time, he won 192 games and struck out 2,590 batters. He won the AL Cy Young Award in 1986, 1987, and 1991. He was also the AL MVP in 1986.

Roger Clemens won three Cy Young Awards during his 13 seasons with the Red Sox. He also won the MVP Award in 1986.

baseman Bill Buckner lost it. The ball rolled between his legs into right field. Meanwhile, Knight ran from second and jumped onto home plate for the winning run. The Mets won Game 7 two days later.

This loss was more crushing than the Red Sox's other World Series losses. Twice the Red Sox were one strike away from victory. A routine play by Buckner would have sent them to the 11th inning. The image of the ball rolling through his legs defined the Red Sox—and the Curse of the Bambino—for years to come.

The Red Sox remained a competitive team after their

heartbreaking loss. They even reached the playoffs in 1988 and 1990. But they were swept in four games each time. Boggs left Boston in 1993, and Clemens left in 1997. But the 1996 arrival of young shortstop Nomar Garciaparra signaled the beginning of a new era in Boston. He was the AL Rookie of the Year after batting .306 with 98 RBIs in 1997.

The Red Sox traded for reigning Cy Young Award winner Pedro Martinez in 1998. He helped them reach the playoffs in 1998 and 1999. But they fell short of the World Series both times. The team added outfielder Manny Ramirez in 2001. He was considered to be one of the best hitters of his generation. Despite having so many talented players, the Red Sox fell short of the playoffs in 2000, 2001, and 2002.

That changed when the team signed designated hitter David Ortiz in 2003. The Red Sox still finished second to the New York Yankees in the AL East. But this time they won the wild card. However, their season ended in a heartbreaking loss to Aaron Boone and the Yankees in the ALCS.

The Red Sox came back in 2004 to finally win their sixth World Series. But they did it without Garciaparra. He had been traded to the Chicago Cubs during the season.

Wade Boggs

Wade Boggs played the first 11 of his 18 Hall of Fame seasons in a Boston Red Sox uniform. Few could match the third baseman's ability at the plate—especially early on. Boggs won five batting titles early in his career. He even won four straight from 1985 to 1988. Boggs continued his good hitting after leaving the Red Sox. Before retiring in 1999, Boggs registered his 3,000th hit. He became only the 23rd person to do so.

Pedro Martinez, *left*, and slugger Manny Ramirez helped the Red Sox become one of baseball's best teams in the early 2000s.

The Red Sox have been among the top teams in baseball from 1998 to 2010. They reached the playoffs eight times during that span. However, they only won the AL East once. They finished second an incredible 10 times.

The 2007 season, when Boston won its division title, was a memorable one. Josh Beckett, Daisuke Matsuzaka, and Curt Schilling anchored a strong Red Sox pitching staff.

Other players stepped up to help Ortiz and Ramirez offensively. Veteran first baseman Kevin Youkilis and third baseman Mike Lowell had good seasons, too. Second baseman Dustin Pedroia was the AL's Rookie of the Year.

The Red Sox won the AL East with a 96–66 record to return to the postseason. They swept the Los Angeles Angels of Anaheim in the ALDS. Beckett pitched a complete game shutout in Game 1. Ramirez and Ortiz each had two home runs in the series.

The ALCS against the Cleveland Indians was tighter. The Red Sox trailed three games to one. But strong performances by Beckett and Schilling got them to a Game 7. The Red Sox then easily beat the Indians 11–2 at Fenway Park.

After waiting 86 years for a sixth World Series title, the Red Sox only had to wait three years for a seventh. The Red Sox met the Colorado Rockies in the 2007 Fall Classic. Beckett led the Red Sox to a 13–1 victory in Game 1. There was little drama the rest of the way. Boston swept the Rockies in four games. Lowell was the Series MVP. He batted .400 with four RBIs and a home run.

The Red Sox reached the playoffs again in 2008 and 2009 behind strong seasons by Youkilis and Pedroia. However, they fell short in 2010, when they finished third in the AL East. It was only the second time in eight seasons that the Red Sox missed the postseason.

The Red Sox began as one of baseball's top teams,

Big Papi

David Ortiz is a beloved player in Boston. He began his career with six injury-plagued seasons for the Minnesota Twins. After signing with Boston in 2003, the player known as "Big Papi" emerged as one of the league's premier power hitters. He set a team record when he hit 54 home runs in 2006. Ortiz and Manny Ramirez made for a fearsome tandem in Boston's order for five and a half seasons. Ortiz is also known for his charity work in Boston and his native Dominican Republic.

Daisuke Matsuzaka posted a record of 46–27 in his first four seasons with the Red Sox.

winning five World Series titles before 1918. There were many forgettable seasons and many heartbreaking losses after that. But the two World Series in the early 2000s confirmed that the Red Sox were in the midst of another glory period.

RoY to MVP

Dustin Pedroia was the 2007 AL Rookie of the Year (RoY) after hitting .317 and driving in 50 runs during the Red Sox's World Series season. One year later, Pedroia was the AL's MVP. The second baseman hit .326 with 83 RBIs and 20 stolen bases. He also won a Gold Glove Award that season.

TIMELINE

1901	The Boston Americans are founded with the start-up of the AL.
1901	The Americans win the pennant and represent the AL against the Pittsburgh Pirates in the World Series. They capture the title behind legendary pitcher Cy Young.
1912	The Red Sox's legendary home field, Fenway Park, opens on April 20.
1912	Sparked by Smoky Joe Wood's 34–5 pitching season, the Red Sox win their second World Series, this time over the New York Giants.
1915	The Red Sox defeat the Philadelphia Phillies to win their third World Series. One year later they beat the Brooklyn Robins in the World Series.
1918	Led by pitcher Babe Ruth and his productive bat, the Red Sox defeat the Chicago Cubs to win their fifth World Series. This is the team's last World Series triumph for 86 years.
1920	In a move that haunts the franchise and creates the phrase "Curse of the Bambino," Ruth is sold to the New York Yankees on January 5.
1933	On February 25, Thomas J. Yawkey gains ownership of the Red Sox and spends the next 43 years trying to bring a World Series championship to Boston.
1941	Ted Williams bats .406, becoming the last player in the major leagues to break the .400 barrier for a season.

1946	The Red Sox win their first pennant in 28 years, but lose the World Series to the St. Louis Cardinals in seven games.
1967	In the "Impossible Dream," the Red Sox jump from ninth in the AL to first. But they lose to the Cardinals in the World Series. Outfielder Carl Yastrzemski wins the Triple Crown by leading the AL in batting average, RBIs, and home runs.
1975	Carlton Fisk hits a walk-off home run in extra innings to keep the Red Sox alive in the World Series. But the Red Sox lose to the Cincinnati Reds in the seventh game.
1978	In a one-game playoff for the AL East title, the Yankees' unheralded shortstop Bucky Dent hits a weak home run over the Green Monster. The Red Sox go on to lose the game and miss out on the playoffs.
1986	The Red Sox reach the World Series and are twice within one strike of the title. But a routine ground ball rolls through Bill Buckner's legs and the New York Mets hold on in Game 6. The Mets eventually win the Series.
2004	The Red Sox come back from a 0–3 deficit to upset the Yankees in the ALCS and then sweep the Cardinals in four straight games to win their first World Series in 86 years. The relaxed group of players call themselves "idiots."
2007	Red Sox fans have only a short wait to enjoy a seventh World Series victory, this time in a four-game sweep over the Colorado Rockies.
2010	The Red Sox finish third in the AL East, missing the playoffs for only the second time in eight seasons.

FRANCHISE HISTORY

Boston Americans (1901–07)
Boston Red Sox (1908–)

WORLD SERIES
(wins in bold)

1903, **1912**, **1915**, **1916**, **1918**, 1946, 1967, 1975, 1986, **2004**, **2007**

AL CHAMPIONSHIP SERIES
(1969–)

1975, 1986, 1988, 1990, 1999, 2003, 2004, 2007, 2008

DIVISION CHAMPIONSHIPS
(1969–)

1975, 1986, 1988, 1990, 1995, 2007

KEY PLAYERS
(position; seasons with team)

Wade Boggs (3B; 1982–92)
Roger Clemens (SP; 1984–96)
Dom DiMaggio (OF; 1940–42,
    1946–53)
Bobby Doerr (2B; 1937–44, 1946–51)
Carlton Fisk (C; 1969, 1971–80)
Fred Lynn (OF; 1974–80)
David Ortiz (DH; 2003–)
Mel Parnell (SP; 1947–56)
Rico Petrocelli (SS; 1963, 1965–76)
Jim Rice (OF; 1974–89)
Ted Williams (OF; 1939–42,
    1946–60)
Carl Yastrzemski (OF; 1961–83)
Cy Young (SP; 1901–08)

KEY MANAGERS

Bill Carrigan (1913–16, 1927–29):
    489–500; 8–2 (postseason)
Terry Francona (2004–):
    654–480; 28–17 (postseason)

HOME PARKS

Huntington Avenue Grounds
    (1901–11)
Fenway Park (1912–)

* Statistics through 2010 season

On June 23, 1917, pitcher Babe Ruth threw four balls in a row to the Washington Senators' lead-off hitter Ray Morgan. Ruth thought a couple of his pitches were strikes and he yelled at home-plate umpire Brick Owens. When Ruth charged Owens and hit him on the neck, Ruth was thrown out of the game. The Red Sox brought in right-hander Ernie Shore. What followed was one of the most unbelievable developments in baseball history. Morgan was caught stealing, and then Shore got the next 26 Senators out. Shore's achievement in the 4–0 win was proclaimed to be a perfect game, since he never allowed another base runner over his nine innings. Decades later, however, a panel of Major League Baseball experts redefined perfect games and disqualified this one from the list because a player had already walked.

"Funny, you never go up there thinking you're going to be hit, and then in a fraction of a second you know it's going to happen. When the ball was about four feet from my head, I knew it was going to get me."—Tony Conigliaro

"Welcome to the most beloved ballpark in America."—Fenway Park public address announcer at Red Sox home games

On September 28, 1960, in the last at-bat of his career, Ted Williams hit a home run off of Baltimore Orioles pitcher Jack Fisher. It was the 521st home run of his career. The 10,000-plus fans at Fenway Park roared as Williams ran around the bases and kept up their applause as he ran into the dugout. There was hope he might step back out and tip his cap, but Williams did not acknowledge the cheers. Novelist John Updike, reporting for the *New Yorker* magazine on October 22, took note of the occasion in an article headlined "Hub Fans Bid Kid Adieu." In part it read, "Gods do not answer letters."

GLOSSARY

ace

A team's best starting pitcher.

designated hitter

A position used only in the American League. Managers can employ a hitter in the batting order who comes to the plate to hit instead of the pitcher.

doubleheader

Two games played in the same ballpark on the same day.

pennant

A flag. In baseball, it symbolizes that a team has won its league championship.

postseason

The games in which the best teams play after the regular-season schedule has been completed.

rival

An opponent that brings out great emotion in a team, its fans, and its players.

rookie

A first-year player in the major leagues.

sportscaster

An announcer who describes or talks about sporting events on television or radio.

veteran

An individual with great experience in a particular endeavor.

wild card

Playoff berths given to the best remaining teams that did not win their respective divisions.

FOR MORE INFORMATION

Further Reading

Boroson, Melinda. *86 Years: The Legends of the Boston Red Sox*. Waltham, MA: Brown House Books, 2005.

Snyder, John. *Red Sox Journal, Year by Year & Day by Day with the Boston Red Sox Since 1901*. Cincinnati, OH: Emmis Books, 2006.

Wisnia, Saul. *For the Love of the Boston Red Sox*. Lincolnwood, IL: Publications International, 2009.

Web Links

To learn more about the Boston Red Sox, visit ABDO Publishing Company online at **www.abdopublishing.com**. Web sites about the Red Sox are featured on our Book Links page. These links are routinely monitored and updated to provide the most current information available.

Places to Visit

City of Palms Park
2201 Edison Avenue
Ft. Myers, FL 33901
617-482-4SOX (4769)
mlb.mlb.com/spring_training/ballpark.
jsp?c_id=bos
City of Palms Park has been the Red Sox's spring-training ballpark since 1993.

Fenway Park
4 Yawkey Way
Boston, MA 02215
617-226-6666
mlb.mlb.com/bos/ballpark/index.jsp
This has been the Red Sox's home field since 1912. Tours are available when the Red Sox are not playing.

National Baseball Hall of Fame and Museum
25 Main Street
Cooperstown, NY 13326
1-888-HALL-OF-FAME
www.baseballhall.org
This hall of fame and museum highlights the greatest players and moments in the history of baseball. Wade Boggs, Ted Williams, Carl Yastrzemski, and Cy Young are among the former Red Sox enshrined here.

INDEX

About the Author

Lew Freedman is a longtime newspaper sportswriter who has worked for the *Philadelphia Inquirer*, the *Anchorage Daily News*, the *Chicago Tribune*, and is currently sports editor of *The Republic* in Columbus, Indiana. He has also written many books about baseball. A baseball fan his entire life, Freedman grew up in the Boston area and attended his first Red Sox game with his grandfather when he was nine years old.